Dead Before You Know It

How to Tidy
Your Personal Papers
Before Your Time is Up!

Patricia Woods

Dead Before You Know It©

How To Tidy Your Personal Papers
Before Your Time Is Up!

Copyright© 2013 by Patricia Woods

A Helpful Little Book®
is a registered trademark of Alamo House Publishing.

This publication is designed to provide accurate and authoritative information in regard to the subject matter covered. It is sold with the understanding that the publisher is not engaged in legal, accounting, or other professional service. If legal advice or other expert assistance is required, the services of a competent professional person should be sought. *From a Declaration of Principles Jointly Adopted by a Committee of the American Bar Associate and a Committee of Publishers and Associations.*

Dead Before You Know It
A Helpful Little Book®

Alamo House Publishing
5804 Babcock Road #322
San Antonio, Texas 78240

alamohousepublishing@gmail.com

www.patriciawoodsbooks.com

This book is dedicated first of all to my children: David, Brianna and Phil.

This book is also dedicated to my family members who actually put their affairs in order. Those precious family members taught me a valuable lesson about loving your family enough to do the right thing, even when it feels uncomfortable. To all who read this book, go out and do likewise for the people you love in your life. Love your family and leave a wonderful legacy, not a legal mess.

TABLE OF CONTENTS

INTRODUCTION

DOCUMENTS YOU NEED before you die? Do we really need a book about that? Apparently we do because so many of us just can't manage the task of gathering essential papers. You bought this book because you need help to get your life in papers in order. Your life in papers is all the paperwork that pertains to your life. That much is obvious on the surface, but it is what lies beneath the surface we must tackle. Those are all the things you will get to one of these days, when you have time. Regardless, you know your important papers should be organized "in case something happens."

> **This book will help you give your family a great gift and legacy: a simple place to find the things they will need when you die.**

The first guarantee I can give you is that something will happen. That something is called death and it will happen to everyone who is alive, sooner or later. You know this is the truth, but if you are like so many people, you haven't really put all your information in order because somehow that might forestall the inevitable. Or whatever it is you think. Some folks are superstitious and think if they avoid thinking or talking about death, it will not really happen, at least to them. Now, you know better than that! Have you met anyone who walked in the Garden with Adam and Eve? Of course not. Then you need to get busy here and you have the first tool in your hands.

This book will help you give your family a great gift and legacy: a simple place to find the things they will need when you die. Your family will grieve your death; they will miss you and feel lonely when you are no longer with them. They will have a grieving process to live through that will be difficult enough. Don't give them a paperwork and financial headache on top of all that. Do them, and yourself, a favor by following some simple steps to gather all your critical papers and information.

Since we have already established the fact that no one gets out of this life alive, a little how-to book on getting out gracefully for the sake of your family seems in order. If you care about your family, and I assume that you do, the things you do now to be organized will save them time, frustration and money later on. You might not hear this when you are still alive, but they will thank you over and over again later on if you put your paper trail in some order. When you do this, you will also be setting an excellent example for your children to follow. Think of this as a family legacy: in your family, you, as the parent, put your affairs in order so your children can spend their time missing you instead of bemoaning your lack of planning and selfishness. Oh, did I strike a nerve there? Good! I meant to! It is selfish to ignore your obligations to the family. Take care of those duties now and then relax knowing you have done your best.

But first, a disclaimer:

While this is a serious topic, I choose to use a light touch for purposes of this book about common sense tasks and simplification. If you want deadly serious talk, go visit your lawyer about your will, which you will have to do, as you well know. I am not a lawyer. I am not giving you legal advice. I am not a financial planner. I am not giving you financial advice. What I am is a writer and a person who has dealt with death in my own family. I have discussed these problems with my friends as all of these topics have come up in our lives with our own families. This work is the result of research, interviews, and personal experience. We all have to face this topic of death, dying and wills, yet we can do so in a way that is not fraught with terror.

The job of organizing your paperwork is not going to take months or years. The length of time it will take depends upon how much you have to accomplish due to the complexity or simplicity of your life. When you own a business, or multiple businesses, things will take more time to assess. The basic principles apply whether your estate consists of the items in one room or a mansion or two. If you have a complicated life, many assets and own several businesses, you can hire people to help you manage. You can hire someone to help you with your paperwork as well. In fact, since most Americans aren't really extremely wealthy entrepreneurs, this is just the right book to help you sort it all out. Good luck and know you are doing the right thing.

The Essentials

♦ **The Big Three Categories**

MOST AMERICANS ARE SO uncomfortable talking or thinking about death and dying I thought some humor might defuse the anxiety you might be feeling. A laugh will help. And a laugh will help you remember to do these things. We tend to avoid things that are unpleasant or make us feel awful about ourselves. So this won't be a scold book: I am not your mother telling you how to behave. Think of me as someone who has lived through some of these things and has some tips to make your life simpler. There, don't you feel better already?

If you are in the baby boomer age group, my guess is that you have already had some experience with at least some of these issues. Your parents might have left things in a mess for you, or perhaps, if you were lucky, they did organize things. My friends have given me lurid examples of messes caused by their parents' lack of planning.

You probably know some horror stories yourself; but our purpose here is to make sure your own life is organized. There might be some loose ends out there your parents didn't have in their own lives, but for you in your life, we will tie those up easily.

For instance, your parents might or might not have had more money, but you have a footprint that is much larger than theirs if you are online, still working, belong to a church, have volunteer jobs or even neighbors who depend upon you. You are most likely far more connected to people outside your neighborhood than your parents were in their lives. There is a simple reason for that: we live very differently now. Because of that, you have much more "stuff" to deal with in the present and that will continue into the future. Do yourself and your family a favor: get all that stuff, really paperwork, organized in one place.

Next up, I have already told you the major disclaimer: my advice is not legal or financial. It tends to be more like the common sense angle of a good friend or family member. This handy guide is for you to have and use as a quick check list for organizing your paper work so your loved ones can find what they need quickly and easily.

The same goes for you while you are still alive to arrange all your papers and then maintain them. If there are too many papers in the file drawer, or not enough, it can cause headaches, confusion and problems when people die. Instead of leaving a mess for your family, keep your life paperwork organized, up to date, and easily accessible. It is one of the best gifts you can give your survivors. We all leave behind a paper trail. Make sure yours is easy to read and use. It also helps in your life now if you can put to hand any important paper without spending hours rifling through the files.

This won't be an arduous task. Most of what I am going to tell you should strike you as sensible, and ultimately doable. These are straight-forward suggestions and ideas for keeping yourself together in real time and online. This is a major area of difference between your life and your parents' lives. I would be willing to bet their online lives were minor or nonexistent. The same can't be said for you, and especially not for your children and grandchildren. It is a brave new world out there, so get ready for some steps to handle that online persona of yours.

In the past people could write a simple will to settle their affairs. Or they could give oral instructions to family members if there was little property involved. For some people, unless there was a substantial amount of money or land involved, a will seemed unnecessary. Life is too complicated now to rely on those two methods. We have bits and pieces of our lives everywhere. Because we also have many critical elements of our lives online, we have technological issues to address with the paper shuffling.

If you are like most people you have email accounts, online banking, investing, perhaps even websites and other footprints across the Internet. All these things have to be taken into consideration when you pull together your files. But I promise it won't be a difficult task, nor will it take months of your life to finish.

The point of having something such as this book as a helpful guide is to keep this process of sorting your life bits as short and simple as possible. Most of us would rather not spend days putting something together. That seems to be the primary reason we postpone pulling the information into one place. We think it will take too long, it's too dreary or scary or boring or whatever. This will be, I promise, a painless process. Well, relatively painless. Easier than playing golf, harder than sleeping. And the payoff will be huge for you and your family when all is said and done.

I will give you a list of things to find and suggest a place to put the items. It will take less time than you imagine, be less painful than you think now, and this exercise will help you stay organized because everything will have "a place to live," so to speak. When your task is complete you will feel like an accomplished person and you can pat yourself on the back. You will also have the satisfaction of knowing you helped your family get through a difficult time with a minimum of fuss. That is another guarantee!

There are practical legal matters you must consider and you need advice from a lawyer, one who will write your will for you. If you have any money at all it is obvious that you have to ask intelligent questions of a tax accountant, a financial planner, an investment advisor or stock broker. The financial decisions you make have consequences. Whether or not you decide to put your assets into a family trust has tax ramifications for your heirs. Your children won't want to deal with probating your estate if it is disorganized or you die intestate, no matter how small the estate, and you don't really want to give too much of your money away in taxes. There are legitimate ways to protect your financial assets that can best benefit your family, friends or charitable institutions.

What if you aren't wealthy or have few financial assets to disperse? Don't worry; we will cover the things that will be most helpful to you. If you have little to spare in material possessions, you still have things to give to someone. You will want to do the right thing no matter what you own.

> **I don't know about you, but I can't keep abreast of the tax and inheritance laws, never mind the peculiarities of investment and dividend income. There isn't enough time in the day to keep up with everything.**

This book can give you assistance in most areas, but you still must hire legal and financial professionals to plan your finances if you have any money at all. The reasons you hire them is that they can shoulder this big burden for you and give you the benefit of their wisdom and experience. Professionals know what has to be done, what can give you the best benefit for your money, and how to put your mind at ease with all the results of your decision making. Financial decisions are intimidating for most of us because we lack the knowledge and experience to stay current with all the rules, changes in markets, and the ability to forecast long-term effects. While you can certainly manage much of your own portfolio with some sage advice, tax laws and the value of money are in constant flux. I don't know about you, but I can't keep abreast of the tax and inheritance laws, never mind the peculiarities of investment and dividend income. There isn't enough time in the day to keep up with everything. Enough said on that.

When you do hire someone, find people who are trustworthy advocates in the legal and financial fields. If you really don't know who to call, ask for recommendations from people who are satisfied with the help they receive from their advisors. Your family or friends probably know some people they have used for these financial and legal services. You won't regret hiring competent, honest professionals. It will save you money and time in the long run. Remember that you want really good people who will do a great job for you so you can feel confident about your decisions. That type of peace of mind is very nearly priceless. And that peace of mind is part of the impetus for making sure your files are in complete order.

Finally, don't be afraid to embark on this journey. It is a journey, not a punishment! The long term benefits far outweigh any short term loss of television viewing time or whatever it is you do with spare hours in the day. Also, you have this book to help you reach your goals. And you need the help, I know. Because as quickly as life continues to fly, you will be dead before you know it!

The Big Three Categories

Where do I put all this stuff?

There are three general categories for files: personal, proof of ownership and financial information. Why did I choose these three? It is much easier to remember how to organize your papers when you put them into three major categories. We can generally hold three categories in our minds without undue strain.

If you like to keep extensive file divisions, you can certainly subdivide these areas to your heart's desire. For the people who have fewer things to manage or hate paperwork, at least this gives you a solid foundation. You can add more files within files if you want, or stick to the basics. Flexibility is the key for your body, mind and files.

The first category is personal information. This includes all that personal information about you, your medical care and conditions, and your identity. It also contains information for your online identities and websites. A digital identity requires access to accounts and websites with usernames, passwords, and so on.

> **Debts do not necessarily die with you, in case you didn't know.**

The second category is about proof of ownership, or in more technical terms, assets and liabilities. This would be all the things you own. From the car to the house, the boat, the swing set, whatever. Any life insurance policies go here because they are an asset to your family and you own them (the insurance policies, not your family!) It also includes your debts, if you have any outstanding, or any paperwork regarding any other debts that you have to, or want to, keep for awhile. The paperwork, I mean, not the debts. This might also include people who owe you money that needs to be collected upon your death, or terms of the loan after your death, or for the disbursal of your financial assets. If someone owes you money, does that have to be paid back to the estate before the estate can be settled? You need to make this information clear and concise.

Debts do not necessarily die with you, in case you didn't know. Not only do big ticket items such as mortgages have to be paid, but car notes and other loans are still due to the lender unless you have insurance that pays off the loan. Be sure to find out what financial obligations are entailed regard your debts in case you die before the debts are paid in full. This is a problem that won't go away on its on, so be sure to take care of it.

The last category is for finances. This is all about the money, regardless of how much or how little you possess. This is where you place the records of your bank accounts, safe deposit boxes, investments, pensions, all those financial things. Here are the details about your financial life that continue until your estate is settled.

In reality, these three broad areas are for finding, keeping and organizing your papers. Once you put these papers together in a sensible way, it will be easy to stay on top of them. Most of your documents will fall into one of these areas. For the truly compulsive, you can amend, expand, refine and fiddle with this list to your heart's content.

These three categories will help you find a specific place to file your paperwork in a way that makes sense to you and your family members or Executor. The beauty of this system is that it is flexible. You can add or subtract as necessary according to your own life and needs. It should be obvious that people who have large families, who have large estates with many assets, or who own businesses, will have more complicated systems. They might need more than half a dozen file folders! Yet, everything can still be summed up in the three main areas.

Finally, have a chat with your investment advisor, accountant, or lawyer about the pile of documents. He or she might want to suggest something else if you have unusual circumstances or are especially blessed with great gobs of money. In the end, this system is supposed to serve you, not the other way around. To that purpose, you will want to remember who's in charge.

Will I or Won't I?

Did you know that up to 70 percent of Americans die without a will? Read that again...up to 70 percent[1]. In a recent survey, half of all Americans with children under 18 have no will[2]. Are all these people stupid or lazy or just like to gamble? Probably not, in most cases, although peo-

---

[1]Hill, Christopher P., 70 Percent of Americans die Without Leaving Behind a Will: What An Opportunity!, *FuneralResources.com*
[2]Scherzer, Lisa, Half of Americans With Kids Set to Die Without a Will, *The Exchange*, Finance, Yahoo.com, 2013

ple can be foolish and careless about providing for their children. As you know, we are reluctant to discuss death. We behave as though talking about death will kill us. To die without a will, especially if you have minor children, is abdicating your parental responsibility. So don't do it.

What happens if you die without a will? A process called intestate succession takes effect. This means the state will draw up a plan for you according to the laws in your state. This plan will then distribute your possessions and wealth to your closest relatives in an equitable manner. Any other distribution you might have envisioned is irrelevant. Your family will get more or less equal distribution, whether that is fair or desirable or against any verbal promises you might have made. Under the provisions of the 1990 Uniform Probate Code, your closest relatives will inherit your property. The shares of the estate will be divided according to your surviving spouse, children, grandchildren, and so on through a specific set of relatives. If there are no close relatives in the specific hierarchy, the state (government) will take the entire estate. If you are unmarried, childless, with no nieces or nephews, but intend to leave your estate to a third cousin, for example, you better write that will now. Otherwise the estate will pass out of your family's hands and into the state coffers. Yes, I am absolutely serious.

If you have no will, you create another problem. The tax burden will quickly become onerous for your surviving family members. As the so-called Death Tax was reinstituted in 2013, the taxes rose on your estate even before you died. If you make sufficient provisions in advance of your death, you can save your family some of your hard-earned money. These issues can best be discussed with your tax attorney, financial planner, banker, or investment advisor. Get sound advice on all your financial matters. It makes a monetary difference for your family. If you are extraordinarily stubborn, just take this advice from me: In some states, in a pinch, you can write a will in your own handwriting on a napkin, have it witnessed and signed by two people, which will make it a legal document accepted by the courts. That will give your family a better chance at saving some money. There is no reason not to do at least that much. However, there is a catch here, these holographic wills, as they are known, are not universally accepted. You still some advice on this from someone qualified to give you the correct information. Generally you can ask this simple question of an attorney and get the answer without being charged. Remember, I do not give legal advice. That's why you have a lawyer.

Now we can move on to the crux of the matter, what to find, gather and file, where to file it, how to file it, and who needs your information.

CATEGORY ONE: Personal Information

♦ **Personal Life Papers**
♦ **Your Online Life**

SO JUST EXACTLY what papers do you need in your files? First in line is the letter of instruction to your executor, a copy of your will and your trust documents. These items are the most important for your family, executor and attorney or financial institutions.

There is another document that should be at the front of your VIP (Very Important Papers) file: a list of people to be notified of your death. This list will be in two parts, first of all family, friends and clergy, and secondly, everyone else. Everyone else is financial institutions, insurance companies, governmental agencies, medical personnel, and any other businesses or institutions with whom you have a relationship. At the end of this book you will find a handy check list. You might want to add more people or tasks to the list as it relates to your circumstances. The people who need to know about your death will be called first and then the process takes on a life of its own. The list will be helpful so people don't find themselves calling the utility company first and the bank last. There is logic and order to the process, which is part of the beauty of it.

Personal Life Papers

It should be fairly easy to understand that you need all the legal papers that identify you. This includes your birth certificate, a marriage license if you are married or a death certificate if your spouse is deceased. If you are divorced, you need a copy of the divorce decree. Likewise, if you remarried, you will need a copy of that marriage certificate. If you have a passport, that needs to be in this file. If you keep your passport in a safety deposit box, include a copy of the pertinent pages identifying you, with a note that the original is in the deposit box. You might want to keep copies of your children's birth certificates as well. Funny things happen to documents and it doesn't really cost anything to make a copy of what you should already possess if your children are younger than 18 years of age. If your children are adults, make sure they have legal copies of their birth certificates. All these pages testify to the fact that you are who you say you are. I am not trying to be clever about this: identity theft is rampant and growing worse. It is no small task to prove who you are when there is another you, or another version of you, out in the world, so to speak. Identity theft is such a problem that an entire industry dedicated to helping you protect your identity has sprung up in the last decade, so keep that in mind when safeguarding your identity. This is the perfect time for me to make a public service announcement: do not give out any personal information to people who call you on the telephone telling you they need your social security number or other confidential data for any reason. Do Not Answer Their Request. There are identity thieves who prey upon people, especially the elderly who tend to be more trusting. Just don't give away any personal information to people who don't need it. Almost no one actually needs your social security number...it is just an easy way to find people. Get some legal advice on this matter. And don't give anyone your information on the phone. NO, NO, NO.

If you or your spouse is a veteran, first of all thank you for your service to this country. Secondly, you should put your entire veteran's information in this file. As you well know, Uncle Sam has certain ways and means of doing things that to the uninitiated seem peculiar. Maybe even more peculiar to those of you who have served. At any rate, you have additional paperwork to file as a veteran (or rather your family will have the work) and things will go more smoothly if you leave them with some instructions. If you plan to have a military funeral or burial, you'd best put that information here also. You are entitled to certain benefits as a veteran, depending upon your length of service. Make all that information available to your family so they will know exactly what to do and whom to contact. If you receive a pension from the mili-

> **...when I started gathering information about my own online life I felt the need for a nap coming on.**

tary, you might as well put that information here rather than in the file with financial matters. Why? It could be less troublesome for your family to handle all the veteran paperwork in one place instead of culling through additional papers. Whatever you decide to do, be sure you explain what your benefits are to your family so they know just what is available for them.

Your Online Life

To me all those papers are easy to gather and maintain. However, when I started gathering information about my own online life I felt the need for a nap coming on. Whew! Let me tell you that my online life might be more hectic than yours because I write and have author websites, author pages on other sites, blog spots, and so on. Your life might not be so overrun with silliness. Or it might be even worse than mine. Don't despair; we can manage this task as well. It just takes a bit of patience and some time.

Let me share with you the process I used to organize my online life. This is the plan I developed and it worked well for me. If it doesn't appeal to you, don't use it. It just suited my way of thinking and working. Because I write out many of my ideas and thoughts by hand in note-books, in a form of journaling, I decided to hand-write some lists so my brain would really function well and I could then check off the sites one at a time. I made a list, in no particular order, of my email accounts, personal and business; my personal or business websites; then the financial institutions I use online; then church related sites, followed by organization sites and hobby or interests sites. I ended with retail sites where I order merchandise.

This turned out to be a rather extensive list for me.

And you will notice that I did not include any contacts, family, friends, or colleagues in this list. The list is based upon websites that I access and for which I must provide a username and password in order to enter the site. Of all the things I did to complete my tasks and be truly organized, this one took the longest and the most work, believe it or not. Writing a will, stating Advanced Directives, issuing personal items to family members...those were easy. My problem is that I got stumped trying to remember my password to seldom used websites!

The good news is this: I made the decision to type up all this information, finally, in a file. The file lists every conceivable place that I visit online and for which I have a user name and password. The list names the site, my user name, and my password. The best part is that now when I forget my password, I can look it up! It also makes it much, much, much easier to change passwords in order to prevent hacking into the account. I no longer have to guess when I last changed my password or what I did before. This is called killing two birds with one stone: you make a list that you can use and so can your executor or your family. Clever, don't you think? Well, I thought it was! It now saves me enormous amounts of time and trouble. Besides, it was embarrassing every time I had to ask T-Mobile what my password was when I wanted to check something in my account. I mean really...how hard can I make these things?

Why am I telling you to make this long list with all that confidential information? The best reason is this: if you do not give your executor or family access to your online presence, they cannot close these accounts without spending a lot of time and energy and some money on it or, conversely, you can't keep an account open for personal purposes. As an example, some people whose family members died couldn't close a Facebook account without producing copies of the death certificate, which makes perfect sense. Remember what I said about identity theft and scam artist? What is the reason for this seemingly inexplicable behavior on the part of the businesses? When you set up an online identity account with a business entity, you have entered into a contractual agreement. Facebook has a contract with *you* for your Facebook page. That does not include your spouse or children. So your family cannot access your account to close it without all the documentation. This gets to be a very complicated problem to solve, depending on which company and what policy.

Businesses that are online have to keep the legal requirements of privacy laws topmost on their minds. Yes, they are in business to make money, but they won't be in business long if they violate these laws. The laws are complicated and designed to protect you, at least in theory. Having said that, it doesn't mean these companies are heartless when you have to deal with a relative's online presence after death. It will, however, be much easier for everyone involved if you take care of these matters now. For instance, you can make provisions in your will to grant access to your family or executor to close your email account with Yahoo, if you have one. Their policies state that clearly. It's a little trickier with other online accounts. But you can solve this problem easily enough with a little research and diligence.

Go to each site where you have an account and read the agreement you signed when you opened the account, or their policies relating to your demise. Find out the proper procedures for dealing with that account when you die. You know Facebook will have a different policy from Twitter. For rather obvious reasons, I might add. Privacy laws were enacted in the mid 1980s, before the advent of the Internet, so there are strict guidelines for protecting you.

Furthermore, you can't actually "will" your digital presence to someone quite the way you would your grandfather's pocket watch. This example might help you

> **Not to be indelicate, but dead people don't buy consumer products, ergo your Facebook page when you die will be a drain on Facebook, not money in their pockets.**

make some sense of your decisions, because you in the digital form have no real substance. Please keep in mind that social media sites exist for business purposes. Although you probably enjoy keeping in touch with family and friends on social media sites, their corporate *raison d'être*, or reason for being, is not to help you talk to your cousins. They are in the business of selling advertising. (You didn't know that? Where have you been?) Not to be indelicate, but dead people don't buy consumer products. You are, if you don't mind the pun, a dead weight. Since the social media field is a growing business, with too many possibilities to list here, remember what I mentioned earlier. These sites exist to make money, when you die you don't spend any more money with the advertisers, so you aren't quite as important as people who are actually living. Find out what has to happen now, before you die, to give your family some guidance on how to handle all your sites.

You can find the answers to most of your questions by contacting these businesses via their help function or sending an email if they accept emails. Don't get me started on businesses that don't really want to hear from their customers and send your email to the round file. Just ask intelligent questions about what to do and most places will be glad to help you. If you have other issues, such as a business page somewhere connected to your social media self, you might need more help or advice. Without sounding like a broken record, I want to remind you that when you have complicated legal questions, please ask your attorney. Maybe you have someone on your staff who handles these things for your business. Just find out the right answers for your particular situation. The restrictions on accessing the accounts of people who have died are numerous. You can't expect companies to break any federal wiretapping laws. Please don't let your emotions rule out common sense here in dealing with these concrete issues. After all, when the world changes frequently, it doesn't take much for even these ballyhooed companies to sink beneath the waves and out of sight. When was the last time you saw an Atari computer? Exactly.

You can find the answers to some of your questions online by using search engines. Attorneys know the statutes (laws) for the state where you live and sometimes it is just much easier and quicker to ask an attorney. Remember my job is to help you figure out what you need to know in order to get organized. I don't dispense legal or financial advice. Except to advise you to call the lawyer. (As a matter of full disclosure, I do have two family members who are attorneys, plus several friends who practice law. That's why I know you need to call your own attorney!)

One last little item: funeral arrangements. This area will be covered in the last chapter, but for now just know that everything pertaining to your final arrangements will be in this first category file. That way no one has to rummage around looking for what you intended. Death sometimes brings up peculiar ideas about funerals. It could also precipitate a family quarrel, so plan your funeral yourself, just to save on the family's emotions.

CATEGORY ONE: More Personal Information

◆ Healthcare and Medical Confidential Information

WITH ALL THE NEW privacy laws in place this is another minefield through which you have to maneuver yourself. Due to regulations established by the federal government and differing state laws, your medical information cannot be shared unless you specifically request this in writing. If you become incapacitated due to illness or an accident, your children have no right to question your doctor about any of your health issues that do not pertain to the immediate crisis. In plain English, no one will tell the family anything about you unless you give permission for them to know. This can cause more problems, bad outcomes, and inevitably the law of unintended consequences will come into play if you do not solve this dilemma well in advance of a crisis.

You can assign one or more family members the task of knowing about your medical conditions. You also have to make some decisions about a Durable Health Care Power of Attorney, sign a Release of Medical Information Authorization form, and fill out a Do Not Resuscitate form, if applicable, and any medical sustainability or end of life forms. These are vital forms and information for your family.

Again, in plain English, you have to decide who you want to make medical decisions for you in case you can't express your wishes. You have to decide whether and how you want your life sustained in the face of a life-threatening illness, condition or accident. If you have a heart attack, chances are you want people to try to save your life. If you have end-stage renal failure, you might want to be kept comfortable rather than having extraordinary measures taken to save you. See my point? What happens if you have a stroke but can survive? What if you suffer from massive brain trauma from an accident or a stroke, leaving you essentially dead unless you are hooked up to medical equipment? I know you don't want to think about it, but these are important decisions. And truthfully, it just is not right to leave your poor children in the lurch wondering what you really want. Lack of information about this has caused rifts in families about what to do with dear old dad who is in a vegetative state with no brain function, kept on the machines, while the children argue about it. Do not do this to the people you love. You would not want it done to you, either.

In my own experience, deciding whether or not to take someone off life-support was very wrenching. Each person's life and case is different, so your family needs to understand your wishes very clearly. I will repeat that: your family needs to understand your wishes very clearly. Write out what you want done so there is no misunderstanding or hard feelings among the siblings.

A family I know had a series of terrible decisions to make when a family member had a stroke. A stroke that can leave you unable to care for yourself and communicate might be someone's idea of living hell. Other people place a high value on the sanctity of life, no matter how imperfect it might be. Make a decision about what you desire, and then write it out clearly and as completely as possible. Take it one step farther and discuss it with your family members or executor, whoever will make the final decisions. Make yourself clearly understood to all the people who will have to make decisions for you. It's the least you can do.

Advanced Directives contain both a living will and the power of attorney, sometimes combined into one document in several states. You can obtain some of these forms online or from some agencies, perhaps even a law library at a law school nearby. Check with your physician's office to find out where they suggest getting forms in the city where you live. You don't necessarily need legal advice to fill out these forms. These forms, all filled out, could save some agonizing decisions for your family. You never know if you will be alive but incapacitated. Do yourself and your loved ones a favor and fill out these forms.

Chapter

4

CATEGORY TWO:

♦ **Proof of Ownership**

AFTER ALL THE STRESS of making those medical decisions and such, this section will be much easier for you. Since this is not an emotional subject, you should be able to whiz right through here. So here we go. Gather up your papers to prove you own that stuff in the garage, even the garage itself! Or maybe the bank still owns your abode, so be it, just gather the papers.

The file will contain the house deed or mortgage documents, plus any land deeds or mortgage documents for land you are acquiring. This includes any escrow mortgage accounts. If you are clever enough to have purchased cemetery or interment spaces, place those documents of ownership and instructions in the file. A little hint here: if it is financially feasible, go out and buy those things now so your family doesn't have to pay for them later.

Most people own a vehicle, so the vehicle title or loan documents must make it into the file. Be sure to have copies of the vehicle registration here, even if you keep the originals in the vehicle. By vehicle I mean automobiles, motorcycles, boats, houseboats, yachts, what have you. You know what I mean…something that hauls your body from one place to another. No, not horses, silly. But if you own a horse, you have to prove ownership of that as well. See what I mean?

As you gather proof of material possessions, you also need to put all your credit card and bank loan documents in the pile here. These pages will testify to any items you are in the midst of purchasing. Ask the tax accountant if a current yearly summary will do the trick and how many years back this information has to go. This is also the place where you need to file the proof of loans made by you and debts owed to you. In other words, if you loan your brother or grandson money to start a business, the paperwork on that loan should appear here. Small family loans don't have to be here. Substantial loans should be, especially as they affect the value of the estate. Go ask the accountant or attorney what to do if it's complicated. If you loaned your children money for food, don't bother to list it here. For heaven's sake, you are supposed to help your children!

If you have life insurance policies they will be in this file. Why? Because you own them and the insurance company has to pay out the value to your family when you die. The amount paid depends upon whether you have a whole life policy or a term life policy along with several other considerations. Just have the paperwork here with the agent's contact information, if possible, but at the very least with the insurance company and policy information.

> **One little note to parents of minor children:
> your surviving spouse will need immediate access
> to some cash and ongoing financial support while your
> death and estate is being handled.**

Finally, any other financial transactions I might have overlooked go here. The next section will include all the really juicy financial information, so you have that to look forward to in a bit. Now, wasn't this much easier than all that deciding about your medical care and funeral arrangements? I told you it would be!

One little note to parents of minor children: your surviving spouse will need immediate access to some cash and ongoing financial support while your death and estate is being handled. Make absolutely certain you have done everything in your power to ensure your spouse can provide for the family adequately while all the details surrounding your death are processed. This is especially true if you are a male and the sole breadwinner, or even if your wife works. Don't leave your family in a financial lurch.

Same song, fifth verse or so, ask your accountant, your lawyer, your financial advisor, your banker, ask somebody to help you make sure your family doesn't go hungry or homeless due to something you did or didn't do. Thank you.

CATEGORY THREE: Financial Information

♦ **Financial Documents**

♦ **Secret Treasures**

HERE COMES THE FUN part of this exercise. Really, you have to believe me on this. Think about everything you have accomplished so far: you set up your files, found all the paperwork you need to prove who you are and everything people need to know about you. You have figured out how someone will make decisions to help you when you are ill, plus you asked that person to be your decision maker and discussed all your wishes with him or her. You have given them permission to take care of you if you can't care for yourself. And you made it clear how you want to be treated if you are very ill.

You love your family, so you wrote a will. Writing a will that specified particular disbursements would help avoid difficulties later. For instance, you made sure your musical daughter got the piano and your book-loving son got the library. Your grandchildren are provided for as individuals with personal items of yours and you left a little something for them to use for education purposes or a down payment for a house, or maybe just enough to buy an elegant meal to enjoy in your name. These instructions clearly spell out your intentions to your family.

The last thing you tackled was gathering together all the deeds and or mortgage documents, vehicle titles, loan papers and then insurance policies. Dry work, but it was easy to do. This next job will be a little bigger than the last one, but not difficult for you. You're becoming an organizational professional at this point. Now it's time for you to place your financial documents together.

Financial Documents

We are going to begin with the obvious things first and work our way down to the more obscure or easy to over look items. The very first thing you want is a list of your bank accounts and the account numbers. You needn't bother about balances since they fluctuate daily and aren't really relevant to this. List every bank account you own. If you have a safety deposit box, list that, its location and number, along with the identification procedures to access the box. You must also make arrangements granting access to your deposit box after your demise. Go to the bank and take care of that this week. The bank will be happy to instruct you on the best way to make these arrangements. Best of all, they won't charge extra for talking to you about all these tasks.

If you have investment accounts you must provide their location (in other words, what investment company you use and if they have a local office) and account numbers. It might also be helpful to list your financial advisor's name with this paperwork, even if you have already listed his or her name elsewhere. It really is convenient to have the contact person's name with the paperwork just as a reminder to people. Every little courtesy helps.

If you have a business and business agreements and investments, that information goes in this file. Be sure to provide all the pertinent paperwork if you are financially involved in a business. If the paperwork is extensive, write a documentary note for this file and place all the business paperwork in a separate file that you can place with these three Very Important Papers file. Don't mislay or lose your business file in the general files in your office. That would negate some of the good work you have done with the other files.

The next items you will need are income statements. If you are still working, this is where you can put your paycheck stubs. I don't really know how many you need to keep in the file, so you should ask your accountant. You can have a back-up file of paycheck stubs. Maybe you only need to keep one year at a time in your major file since that is the most up to date information about your income from work.

And of course you have to keep current tax information. Your file will contain the most recent tax returns, say for the last year or so, with the leftovers in another file your family can actually find!

As you can clearly tell at this point, there are some files that have to be cleared out and updated yearly. This is not news, just as you know you don't need tax documents from 20 years ago. This helps you cut down on extraneous paperwork that clutters up your home. Simply put, when you keep your files current, you eliminate messy files and a paper fire hazard.

Secret Treasures

Secret Treasures, as I like to call them, are things that

don't necessarily fit in other places. It must seem that there can't be any place left to stick something, but you're not quite finished here. Someone else might call this the miscellaneous section, but that is a really boring way to describe this. Let's just say there might be one or two odd things that don't particularly fit so neatly elsewhere. Not your retirement stuff, that's the next chapter, but some other little thing I didn't think of but you thought of instantly. It would be your little secret treasure, no matter how simple it might be. This is, of course, about financial things, not about your silver brush and comb dresser set that came from your five greats grandmother. There are always some little things that just don't seem to belong in a particular place. You will recall that the last time you moved and opened a box marked kitchen stuff and found a little something that didn't belong in the kitchen, you wondered what on earth you were thinking when you packed the box. This is like that. If you have some leftover financial items, put them here. At least they will be with like-minded papers. After all, if it's about money, it doesn't belong with your birth certificate. That should be all I need to say on that.

CATEGORY THREE: More Financial Information

♦ **Retirement and Insurance Information**

IF YOU HAVE an Individual Retirement Account and or a pension, your paperwork slides right into the file here. As usual, make sure you have all the information about your account, the account numbers, and contact information for the people who must be notified of your death. If there are any special procedures to follow, make note of them for the file so you can discuss them with your family or executor. Different policies might require different ways of handling information, so include as much as you can.

For those of you with annuity contracts or 401 (K) accounts, the same advice applies. List your accounts, their location, account numbers and contact information for notification purposes. Any additional information about the policies that are necessary should be filed with the rest of the paperwork here. My advice is don't separate the policies from the rest of the information. It is easy to over-look things when trying to make sense of filing.

Health insurance policies should be kept here, because once you die, you won't need to pay premiums. Your insurance company should be notified fairly early in the process in order to stop any automatic payments that might be coming out of your checking account.

The same holds true for any Long Term Care insurance or Disability insurance policies. Not to belabor the obvious, but unless you are alive and kicking, you won't be needing these services! Your family or executor will want to cease any outgoing payments that are unnecessary as soon as possible. Your executor or family members need to know if there will be any reimbursement or disbursement of funds expended on these little items. Keep all these policies together so they are tidy and can be accessed immediately and easily. Oh yes, once again, tell them about it now while it's on your mind.

If you receive any type of government benefits, that paperwork should be in this file, too. Whether it's Social Security, SSI, disability, or anything else, if it is money that comes to you from a state or federal agency, this information belongs in this file. These are also people who will need to be told of your death and the correct information in the file will help your family or executor. Believe me, the government employees want name, rank and serial number, so to speak. Provide names, date of birth, whatever will be called for when your family makes those telephone calls on your behalf.

Basically everything to do with your retirement, pension, and insurance policies belong together. Since I've already explained about all these people who have to be notified of your death, you know that this will be a time-consuming job for whoever handles all your papers. Placing paperwork and information for contacting the right people together helps the process along. Since all these

Did you know if you open an Individual Retirement Account, an IRA, and don't make a withdrawal from it by age 70½ it is considered dormant and the money lies unclaimed, just like the insurance policies?

items are tied together, your family will have to cancel some payments, reroute others, and generally sweep up all the loose ends. Having everything gathered together makes life better for all the people involved.

Remember that your family members need all the account information for your retirement and insurance policies, the insurance carrier's name, the account and policy numbers, and your agent, if possible. There is a simple reason for this, too.

It might shock you to know that millions of dollars are held by insurance companies because the deceased didn't provide the insurance policy information to family members, the families didn't know about the insurance, so the companies never paid off the policy. These unclaimed policy payments have accumulated to over $500 million in the past *decade*. That is money someone sacrificed to put into a policy to help the family. But they simply forgot to tell their family about the policy. Not really spectacular thinking on that one. There are excellent reasons for keeping track of your important papers. And just by the way, did you know if you open an Individual Retirement Account, an IRA, and don't make a withdrawal from it by age 70½ it is considered dormant and the money lies unclaimed, just like the insurance policies? No one will call up your heirs to remind them that they have money coming to them and they need to claim it! We are talking about *tens of millions of dollars lying unclaimed* here. People foolishly leave money in accounts when they fail to keep track of their investments, policies, accounts and their heirs can't claim the money because they didn't know about it. It is a crying shame for all those families.

WRAPPING IT ALL UP

◆ **A Check List for All**

BY NOW YOU ARE near the end of collecting and filing the information you need. You have met with your attorney and financial advisor, made a trip to the bank and other financial institutions, talked to insurance agents and filled out paperwork. You have made copies of all your important documents and placed them in a safe deposit box. And of course you have discussed your plans and wishes with your sweet family members. They are, after all, the reason you have worked so diligently.

One of the things I have not included in this book is a plan for funeral arrangements. There is a very good reason for that: Gail Rubin has written the definitive book on planning your funeral. Her book, *The Good Goodbye: Funeral Planning for People Who Don't Intend to Die* is a comprehensive work. There is absolutely nothing I can add to her sage advice. I recommend you buy the book and plan your funeral. After all, if you have done everything you can according to the suggestions in this book, much of the hard work is already finished! You now have the freedom to set out the plans for a great funeral for your family and friends to attend.

You love your family and want to give them peace of mind knowing that you have made the necessary arrangements for your funeral. Death can bring on many family quarrels when people have to guess what to do, what the deceased might want, how much money they should spend on final arrangements and the drama continues. Death also brings out guilt, which might cause a family to spend more than they can actually afford on a casket and other items for the burial. You can eliminate these worries by making plans and discussing your wishes with your family.

If you feel uncomfortable talking about these personal decisions with your family, spell them out on paper and discuss them with a clergy person or an attorney. Just be sure you are clear in what you want done with your remains and the service for your family and friends. If at all possible, prepay your expenses. If you want cremation, you can prepay for those arrangements, as well as the interment expenses. You can order a casket of your choosing and pay all those expenses. It will benefit your family to have all these worries taken care of before you die.

If you know what kind of a service you want, you can make specific recommendations for that. Someone such as a clergy person will be happy to help you plan a service. Some churches have someone on staff who helps people plan the service and draws up the paperwork. You might not have strong likes or dislikes, but someone else might. For instance, I have a lengthy list of music and hymns I want to have played at my funeral service. As someone who has played hymns in churches since childhood, I have pretty definite ideas about what I want. It just seemed natural to me to plan a service involving joyful music that I thought would be helpful to my family members. A positive aspect of this is that my children don't have to guess what I want. My hope is the music I chose will lift their spirits and help them in their own faith walk. You can do the same thing for yourself. Perhaps the music isn't that important to you, yet you can understand what I am saying to you. When you make plans for the future, that act can help lessen the anxiety that accompanies a death.

What matters is that you do something about your funeral, whatever kind of funeral you want, which leaves your family to concentrate on something else. It is a much easier task to plan your funeral than to plan your vacation. Think about that for just a moment. Your vacation requires much more work and might even cost more than a funeral. It depends upon your vacation plans and what kind of final arrangements you make. Just don't stress about it. You can do this last little bit, I guarantee it. And that is another real guarantee.

One of the major aspects of this work was to reduce excess paperwork. Many people keep reams of paper that is useless if they are incapacitated or die. Other people don't keep basic paperwork or they file the papers in some way that makes them inaccessible. By now you should not have either one of those problems. If you have any lingering messes, get rid of them. File those papers and be done with it!

The Check List for All at the end of this chapter is designed to help you gather all your papers in an orderly way. You might have additional items that are not on the list or that are specific to your situation. Remember this list is a guide, not something cast in stone, so you can keep track of what you need and what you are doing. It is difficult to invent a list that indicates all the possible items that could be included. Yet the list is a place to start and might even be more than what your situation requires. Use the list and do what you need to do.

This is the end. Not of your life, we hope, but the end of my advice to you. I hope you found this book easy to follow and understand. My sincere hope is that you have taken the best steps you can to make your future, and that of your children, brighter by giving them what you all need to face a difficult time.

We are not eager to face death. By preparing for it at least on paper, we can reduce some of the anxiety. One last guarantee I can give you is that accepting the inevitability of your death will help you live an authentic life now for whatever time you have left. As the Apostle Paul asks in the book of Romans, "Death, where is thy sting?" You have started to remove death's sting. Good luck and enjoy your life!

CHECK LIST FOR ALL...
With Real Places for a Check Mark!

1. Personal Information—From birth to death, including medical

__ Letter of Instructions for Executor and Attorney*

__ List of People to Contact*

__ Birth Certificate

__ Marriage License (and divorce decree, if applicable)

__ Passport

__ Death Certificate of spouse

__ Personal and Family Medical History or information

__ Durable Health Care Power of Attorney

__ Release of Medical Information Authorization

__ Do Not Resuscitate-if applicable

__ Living Will

__ Will

__ Durable Power of Attorney If Applicable

__ Trust Documents

__ Your Online Information

__ Funeral Service Instructions and Information

__ Veterans Information

*Most important papers to place in the front of the file folder.

2. Proof of Ownership—Assets and Liabilities

___ House Deed or Mortgage Documents, Land Deeds or Mortgage Documents

___ Cemetery or Interment Documents and Instructions

___ Escrow Mortgage Accounts

___ Vehicle Titles or Loan Documents

___ Credit Card or Bank Loan Documents

___ Proof of Loans Made and Debts Owed

___ Financial-all the rest of the money information

___ Life Insurance Policies

3. Financials—Everything Not Already Included

___ List of Bank Accounts and account numbers

___ Safety Deposit Box accounts and numbers, with identification procedures

___ Investment Accounts-locations and numbers

___ Business Agreements and Investments

___ Income Statements

___ Tax Returns

___ Individual Retirement Account information

___ Pension Information

___ Annuity Contracts and numbers

___ 401(K) Accounts

___ Health Insurance Policies

___ Long Term Care Insurance or Disability Insurance

___ Government Benefit Papers

Some additional information you might want to include on your list could be adoption papers, if your children are adopted. You can add copies of your diplomas or specify where your diplomas are hanging if you keep them on a wall at home or in your office.

If your family wants to include your work history as part of your obituary, you could include that information here. Not a full resume, for heaven's sake, just the basics. This information could be helpful to your family.

Finally, if you have pets, you have to include some information on your vet, who cares for the pets, and who you want to take your pets. Be absolutely certain you discuss the new living situation of your pets with the new prospective owner. Don't leave it to chance or hope someone will take care of Buffy and Fluffy. Be as considerate of them as you would be any other family member. If you have no family, make arrangements with friends, or state that you want your pets to be adopted by someone. Be as specific as you would with anything else. These are your other family members, so take good care of them.

Make Your Own Check List For Additional Items

_____

_____

_____

_____

_____

_____

_____

_____

_____

_____

_____

_____

_____

_____

_____

_____

Bibliography and Resources

These are some of the resources available to you. When searching online, using a search engine will yield more information than you might want to read. That is, of course, why I wrote this helpful little book!

As I mentioned earlier, the first place to start is a trip to your local financial institution and then on to your lawyer. Legal advice is accurate, timely and, well, legal.

Every state has different laws and your lawyer can tell you exactly what steps you need to take to get your life in order. You need legal help and the proper legal documents. Information on wills, probate, family trusts and other legal matters are best discussed in person with your attorney. Hie thee to the lawyer's office and get the best information you can. It will be well worth the time and money. On the other hand, if you are a dedicated Do It Yourselfer, you can write a will that is legal and binding if it is properly witnessed. Information on writing a simple will is available online. If you really can't even do that, write it down, sign it, have it witnessed, and you have done your duty. That won't work well for people with major assets, but if that's not you, just write down your wishes. If you have some questions, your local library will have reference materials to help you. Just don't let it go. You need a will! Remember your family will thank you.

Your financial advisor can direct you to the best sources for your situation as well. You have to make the necessary decisions about your money and property. As the tax laws change, your situation will change. You can begin with your bank and then move on to your other sources. The resources and bibliography listed here are not exhaustive. The point of this book is to help you get organized, not to overwhelm you. After you finish this work, you can rest easily knowing you've done your best to help the family members who will settle your estate. May you rest in peace.

BIBLIOGRAPHY

Allard, Heather, The Mogul Man, 10 Business Documents You Need, May 9, 2012.

Brixey, Marcia, Tell Your Family You Love Them-Write Your Will, *Forbes*, March 30, 2012, online. Accessed June 24, 2013.

Carroll, Evan and Romano, John, *Your Digital Afterlife When Facebook, Flickr, and Twitter Are Your Estates, What's Your Legacy?* Berkeley, CA: New Riders, 2012

Chaudhuri, Saabira, The 25 Documents You Need Before You Die, *The Wall Street Journal*, July 2, 2011. Print.

FindLaw, Understanding Intestacy: If You Die Without an Estate Plan, *FindLaw.com*. Accessed June 24, 2013.

Fowler, Geoffrey A., Life and Death Online: Who Controls A Digital Legacy, *The Wall Street Journal*, January 5, 2013. Print.

Hill, Christopher P., 70 Percent of Americans die Without Leaving Behind a Will: What An Opportunity!, *FuneralResources.com*, from ProducersWeb.com, 2012. Accessed June 24, 2013.

Rocket Lawyer News, In a New Era of Estate Planning Rocket Lawyer Survey Shows That Only Half of Adults Have a Will, *Rocket Lawyer News*, RocketLawyer.com, March 28, 2012. Accessed June 24, 2013.

Rubin, Gail, *The Good Good-Bye: Funeral Planning for Those Who Don't Plan to Die*. Albuquerque, New Mexico: Light Tree Press, 2010.

Ruff, Howard, 9 Year Mortgage Blog.

Scherzer, Lisa, Half of Americans With Kids Set to Die Without a Will, *The Exchange*, Finance, Yahoo.com, 2013. Accessed June 24, 2013.

Online Resources

There are several online sources for creating your own will. Conduct an Internet search and find the one you prefer.

Social Security information is found at www.socialsecurity.gov.

Veterans' information: www.va.gov.

www.lawyers.com/estate planning/organize your paperwork

www.motleyfool.com—Prepare for your Demise

www.caring.com—Check List for Aging Parents

www.mashable.com—Prepare for your death online

www.webmd.com—Putting Affairs in Order Before Death, Tom Valeo.

Resolute Lawyers and Associates, 10 Documents You Need Before You Die. Blog

Author Acknowledgment

It is true writers require the assistance of many people. I want to thank the people who have helped me bring this book to print.

A great big thank you to Kathy Wagoner for technical work and a yeoman's job of processing. Barbara Blumenfeld, Director of Legal Writing, University of New Mexico School of Law, for all things legal. She gave sage advice. Any and all mistakes are mine, without respect to her guidance. Mark Bussemeier for reading and commenting on the manuscript in view of his daily calling. Thank you for the spiritual advice as well! Sabra Armijo for research and design work and being a willing reader for ages. Cristina Arnold and Kerry Lewis, great people in a difficult business arena, for astute observations and suggestions for now and future work.

Finally, my children get the biggest thank you. Your continuing love and support is vital. I love you all.

About Helpful Little Books®

Helpful Little Books® are just that...helpful and little. This series of books will give you solutions to every day problems, some vital such as the subject of this book, and others designed to help you make wise choices to live better. All the books are short. People are bombarded with too much information they can't possibly access. As the rate of information grows exponentially (that means really, really fast, so fast you have trouble counting) we cannot keep up with the flow of new knowledge. Wise people don't attempt to keep track of it all. Just as we have to choose our battles carefully, we have to choose areas of life that interest us and we want to learn about or that are essential to having better, more enjoyable lives. We simply cannot know everything or do too many things. That means you want simple solutions to your problems as often as possible.

As a pragmatist who believes practical trumps glitz, I believe you want practical solutions, too. This is especially true if you have no money to throw away. Do you actually know people who can throw money away on silliness? No, of course not, so you get my meaning.

These books can help you. That's the bottom line. Now go out and enjoy your life!

www.ingramcontent.com/pod-product-compliance
Lightning Source LLC
Chambersburg PA
CBHW071624170526
45166CB00003B/1187